DISCOVER
HAMMERHEAD SHARKS

by Virginia Loh-Hagan

Cherry Lake Publishing • Ann Arbor, Michigan

3

Published in the United States of America
by Cherry Lake Publishing
Ann Arbor, Michigan
www.cherrylakepublishing.com

Content Adviser: Dr. Jelle Atema, professor of marine biology at
Boston University and adjunct scientist at the Woods Hole
Oceanographic Institution
Reading Adviser: Marla Conn, ReadAbility, Inc

Photo Credits: © Ian Scott/Shutterstock Images, cover; © Gary J. Wood/Flickr
Images, 4; © Ethan Daniels/Shutterstock Images, 6; © Matt9122/Shutterstock
Images, 8, 18; © Jeff Kubina/Shutterstock Images, 10; © Brandelet/Shutterstock
Images, 12; © Don Long/Shutterstock Images, 14; © frantisekhojdysz/
Shutterstock Images, 16; © Volt Collection/Shutterstock Images, 20

Library of Congress Cataloging-in-Publication Data
Loh-Hagan, Virginia.
  Discover hammerhead sharks / by Virginia Loh-Hagan.
    pages cm—(Splash!)
  Audience: Ages 6–10.
  Audience: K to grade 3.
  Includes bibliographical references and index.
  ISBN 978-1-63362-599-0 (hardcover)—ISBN 978-1-63362-689-8 (pbk.) —
ISBN 978-1-63362-779-6 (pdf)—ISBN 978-1-63362-869-4 (ebook)
  1. Hammerhead sharks—Juvenile literature. I. Title.

QL638.95.S7L64 2016
597.3'4—dc23

                          2015005393

Cherry Lake Publishing would like to acknowledge the work of the Partnership
for 21st Century Skills. Please visit www.p21.org for more information.

Printed in the United States of America
Corporate Graphics

TABLE OF CONTENTS

Special Heads

Most hammerhead sharks have heads that look like hammers. Some look like shovels. There are nine **species** of hammerheads.

The head of this shark makes a T-shape.

Their heads make them unique. Hammerheads can make quick, sharp turns. They swing their heads from side to side as they swim. The motion helps the shark **navigate** and stay **afloat**.

CREATE! Imagine what hammerheads would look like if their heads were actual hammers. What about other tools, like wrenches or screwdrivers? Draw your new animal!

The hammerhead's head helps it swim.

Their eyes and **nostrils** are on the sides of their heads. Hammer-heads can see above and below their bodies. But they can't see in front of them. They see and smell better than most animals.

Hammerheads can't see what's in front of them.

Social Sharks

A female hammerhead might have 30 to 40 **pups**. Baby hammerheads have soft, round heads. Their heads **flatten** as they grow. The pups stay together. They leave when they get big.

Baby hammerheads look similar to adults.

Hammerheads travel in **schools** during the day. Each school has hundreds of hammerheads. Schools consist of mostly female hammerheads. They are looking

LOOK!

Look at some photographs or videos of hammerhead sharks traveling as a school. It's amazing to see so many of them in one place. What things do you notice? Share the image with a friend at school!

Hammerheads travel in large groups called schools.

for mates. They **migrate** together. They swim to warm waters.

Hammerheads use body language to talk to one another. They shake their heads. They do fancy body twists. They are the most social kind of shark.

Hammerheads move their bodies to communicate.

Nocturnal Hunters

Hammerheads are **nocturnal**. They leave their schools at night to hunt alone.

THINK! Like other sharks, hammerheads are at the top of the food chain. They have few natural enemies. But hammerheads still face threats. What do you think they are?

Hammerheads hunt for food alone.

Compared to other **predators**, hammerheads have small mouths. But they still have very sharp teeth. They use the **senses** on their heads. They find and eat animals hiding in the ocean floor.

Hammerheads eat small fish, squids, and sometimes even other sharks.

Hammerheads hunt along the ocean floor.

But stingrays are their favorite food. Hammerheads use their heads to pin the stingrays. Their heads help make them great hunters!

Many hammerhead species like to eat stingrays.

Think About It

Hammerhead sharks are known to eat each other. This is called cannibalism. Why do they do this? What other animals do this, and why? Go online to find out.

Like other sharks and predators, hammerheads help keep the oceans healthy. How do they do this?

Out of 100 shark attacks on humans, only three are caused by hammerheads. They normally do not eat humans. But they will attack when angered. Why do you think that is?

Find Out More

BOOK
Stille, Darlene R. *I Am a Shark: The Story of a Hammerhead Shark*. Minneapolis: Picture Window Books, 2004.

WEB SITE
National Geographic Kids—Animals: Hammerhead Shark
http://kids.nationalgeographic.com/animals/hammerhead-shark/
Read some basic facts about hammerhead sharks, and look at some photos.

Glossary

afloat (uh-FLOHT) does not sink

flatten (FLAT-uhn) to become less round

migrate (MYE-grate) to move from one area to another

navigate (NAV-ih-gate) to find one's way over a long distance

nocturnal (nahk-TUR-nuhl) active at night

nostrils (NAH-struhlz) openings to breathe and smell through

predators (PRED-uh-turz) animals that live by hunting other animals for food

pups (PUPS) baby sharks

schools (SKOOLZ) large groups of fish

senses (SENS-ez) smell, sight, taste, hearing, feeling

species (SPEE-sheez) one type, or kind, of plant or animal

Index

About the Author

Dr. Virginia Loh-Hagan is an author, university professor, former classroom teacher, and curriculum designer. She relates to hammerhead sharks because she also has an oddly shaped head. In addition, she's social and nocturnal. She lives in San Diego with her very tall husband and very naughty dogs. To learn more about her, visit www.virginialoh.com.